Cover Photo Taken By:

Mahalia Goodey, Prairie Echo Photography

© 2020 Mahalia Goodey, Prairie Echo Photography

ISBN 978-1-7773254-1-1

ISBN 978-1-7773254-2-8

ISBN 978-1-7773254-3-5

Copyright © 2020 by Megan Ritchie

All rights reserved. No part of this book may be reproduced or used in any manner without written permission of the copyright owner except for the use of quotations in a book review.

Table Of Contents

Dedication	4
Introduction	6
Concerns	8
My Dock Diving Start	13
Three Real World Strategies To Introduce Your Dog To Dock Diving	20
Introducing Your Dog To Water	21
How to find the right natural body of water to start your dog	22
How to avoid injury	34
Introducing Your Dog To Water	44

Building The Foundations For The Dock	51
Introducing Your Dog To The Dock	**60**
A Positive Introduction To The Pool	62
Common Problems & Trouble Shooting	79
Jumping Off The Dock With Confidence	**93**
How To Build Confidence On The Dock	93
Increasing Motivation	110
Now what?	**116**
Resources:	**125**

Dedication

I didn't write this book to make millions and millions of dollars (it won't), but because I believe getting involved in dock diving can change your relationship with your dog.

I understand human nature and I know that a lot of the dog owners who purchase my book just have a passing interest in training their dog to "do something", and will never use any information from this book no matter how valuable it is. However, I know there are a select few who are passionately dedicated to giving their dog the best life possible. Who are dedicated to giving their dog an outlet for their innate doggie desires, who want to put in the effort to strengthen their bond with their dog, and who will stop at nothing to chase down every last resource to help them do just that.

If you fall into the latter category you're going to find the content in this book extremely valuable.

It's my hope that a year or two from now, when you're competing for a National Championship, someone asks you how you got started, and that you can point to this book and say that it got you and your dog hooked on this awesome sport.

So, this book is dedicated to you. Those dedicated few who will take the direction from this book, put it in action, and pursue your dreams for your dog with your whole heart.

Introduction

First, I wanted to say thank you for taking the plunge and picking up this book. Thank you for giving your dog a chance to try this fun sport, and thank you for being the kind of dedicated owner that wants to improve your relationship with your dog. If you've found yourself interested in dock diving but haven't been sure how to start, you've found exactly the right book. By the end of this book you'll know how to introduce your dog to water, how to introduce your dog to the pool in a positive way, and ultimately how to get your dog to take their first jump off the dock…and, of course, learn some trouble shooting tips along the way.

Before we dive too quickly into dock diving, let me introduce myself, my name is Megan Ritchie and I am the owner of High Drive – a specialty sporting dog equipment shop. I am not a professional dog trainer, just a fellow enthusiast who competes and trains in multiple dog sports. I currently own two Curly Coated Retrievers, and am a new dock diving addict. Through this book, I'm looking to recruit fellow addicts to their new favorite sport.

Through this book I'd like to share with you everything I've learnt through various lessons, seminars and webinars, as well as real world experience implementing these tips myself.

In this book I will walk you through how to start your dog – from never seen water before – to preparing for your first trial. Let's dive in!

Concerns

Before we get into the nitty gritty specifics, I want to address some common concerns that might be holding you back and have you thinking you *can't* participate and succeed in dock diving. There's no point in having you worry about it the whole time reading this book, so let's just address them now and get them out of the way!

If you're thinking:

But Megan, my dog doesn't like to swim, they can't dock dive

I hate to say it, but you're wrong. You can. I think we can train our dogs to do just about anything we'd like with enough persistence and encouragement. Now, if you think your dog has no interest in it, maybe it's not the sport for them. However, you'd be amazed how quickly you can teach your dog to love this sport. So, I'd definitely encourage you to give it a try and see if you can turn around their uncertainty and teach them to love this fun game.

If your dog is really struggling with the swimming part, they can wear a doggie life jacket (even in competition). So, if they are still developing confidence around swimming, or just getting their feet wet for the first time, a life jacket can be a great way to introduce this sport.

You can see in this photo of my older dog Tess, she's got her life jacket on, which definitely gives her more confidence when it comes to swimming in the new pool environment – even though she is quite happy to play and swim at the lake without one.

© Mahalia Goodey, Prairie Echo Photography

But Megan, my dog isn't a retriever we can't do well in this sport

You might be surprised to hear it, but retrievers aren't necessarily the best dogs at dock diving. A lot of the world record holders are actually Whippets, lighter and leggier dogs, and purposefully bred Flyball mixes.

So, you definitely do not need a retriever to play this game. Of course, if you have a retriever, they will probably love it! So, never fear, a lot of different breeds participate in this sport, and since competition is geared more towards beating your own personal best vs. beating other dogs entered in the competition, there's no reason to worry about what anyone else is doing. Just focus on your success.

But Megan, I don't have access to a pool, or an instructor we can't learn this sport

Nope, that excuse isn't going to work either, you definitely can. If you have access to a natural body of water you can certainly start to train for dock diving, and even compete. While it wouldn't be ideal to compete with your dog before ever seeing a pool, it is possible. Especially for a more confident dog. Dog's with prior competition experience in other sports are going to have an advantage if you are forced to do it that way, other than the pool the biggest challenge for teams with no prior competition experience is getting used to benching, spectators, judges, and photographers.

But Megan, this might be easy for you to do, you've trained your dog for lots of other things before, but I've never trained my dog for anything. I can't do it.

Everyone starts (any dog training) at the beginning, we all start knowing nothing. You have to start somewhere. This book was written with new handlers in mind, so if you've never trained your dog for any sport before, this is the book for you. I also hope that more experienced handlers will get a lot out of this book, but it's been written to take you from zero to hero!

We're going to walk through exactly how to introduce your dog to each step in a thoughtful and positive way, and go over common training issues you might see and how to fix them.

But Megan, my dog doesn't like toys. We can't play.

You can dock dive too! The more toy motivated your dog is the easier it's going to be to train, but it isn't necessary for introducing your dog to the sport.

Step-by-step we are going to walk through tricks that you can use to introduce your dog to water, even if they don't like toys. We will also discuss how to build that toy drive on dry land and transfer that desire to the water.

My Dock Diving Start

How did I get started dock diving? I actually started in 2016 with my older dog Tess. A training pool had opened up locally, it was not regulation pool but it was built for dock diving.

The pool had a few modifications that made Tess a little unsure with the pool environment, one being that the ramp had some movement to it, which really bothered her. Tess is on the more sensitive side to start, and some of the introduction techniques used didn't make it the most positive introduction for her.

I think one of the reasons that they designed the ramp to move was so they could "force" the dogs to swim in the pool by lowering the ramp so the dogs had to swim back to the ramp rather than taking the extra time to allow them to decide for themselves. For some dogs that wouldn't phase them at all, but for a more sensitive dog like Tess, it was enough to make her not want to participate in the sport.

At the end of the day it just wasn't a great situation for us to practice in and led her to not being too interested in the sport. So, if that was a mistake for a dog like Tess, in this book we're going to discuss what to do instead. There were a few other issues in the way that that business was allowing pool use that made it a challenge for us – they had just opened the pool and were still trying to figure out how to offer pool time, make sure everyone was using it safely, whether to provide instruction and training, how to charge for pool use, all while still running a profitable business.

Like most small businesses they were forced to tinker with their offering to ensure that they could stay profitable while meeting insurance requirements, and making their customers happy. I can't criticize them for that, but with moving goalposts on what was and wasn't allowed at the facility the situation just didn't work for us.

Without instruction I was comfortable with, and accessible pool times available, it was not an ideal situation to get started. I don't remember ever actually making a decision to stop, but there were enough roadblocks in the way that I gave up.

Tess was involved in many sports at the time so it was easy to let it slide and focus on other sports that were easier to participate in. That's one reason I love owning a versatile breed, there are so many opportunities to participate in fun sports with them we can easily move in whatever direction they take us. However, in this case it just made it easy to say this isn't the right situation for us, so we're not going to do it right now.

In 2019 a new dock diving pool was built in a neighboring city (a ninety-minute drive away). The prior pool was in the process of moving to a new location, so that made the new pool the only training option available. While it wasn't super close, it was close enough that we could go practice.

I started seeing videos and photos of friends renting and training at the pool. That desire to try it was starting to creep in again. Online training had becoming more readily available, the American Kennel Club had created some introductory dock diving videos, other YouTube videos and training were more readily available. With more self-teaching resources, I was running out of excuses not to try it again.

One day, scrolling through Facebook I saw that the new pool was offering a training seminar to introduce people to the sport. Since these are so few and far between, I knew I couldn't pass up on the opportunity. They were hosting a trial a few weeks after the seminar, so that created an even stronger desire to register for the seminar right away.

That specific facility is located in a smaller town, but within driving distance of three larger cities, so the seminar format seemed to work really well for them as people could commit to the day fairly easily, compared to the commitment to attending a normal six-week class. However, if you have access to a more regular practice or class that would definitely be an ideal way to get started.

I attended the seminar with my younger dog Riggs, and we got a lot out of it. Riggs is more confident than Tess so I thought he'd be more successful within the timed constraints of a seminar. The seminar was an extremely positive and welcoming environment; however, I find anytime there is a time constraint like competing or a seminar you feel that subconscious pressure to get more accomplished because you only have a short period of time to see success.

If you've watched our Dog Sports Decoded podcast, I did a really interesting interview with the seminar instructor Gulnaz Zagidullina. She's such a wealth of knowledge and in both the seminar and the podcast she shared such great insight on getting a dog started in dock diving; a lot of that information has influenced my thinking in writing this book. It really gave me the confidence to get going in dock diving and start to practice on our own.

I also signed up for an online dock diving class through Fenzi Dog Sports Academy, which I can't recommend enough. I got a few more drills and ideas from that class, and wanted to incorporate those ideas into this book as well.

After absorbing what all these resources taught and knowing the first trial was quickly approaching, I wanted to get a few more practices in. At that point, I had only done training with Riggs, but I hate leaving Tess out of fun things like this, so I wanted to see if she would have a renewed interest in the sport. In order to get that extra practice in I decided to rent the pool with a few friends.

Due to Riggs' confident nature we saw success pretty quickly at our first seminar, with him jumping off the dock in the first ten minutes of pool time. I knew with Tess our progress wouldn't be quite that quick. She already had a negative first impression at the other pool, and she's more sensitive by nature. I did not think Tess would be ready to jump off the dock for the upcoming trial, so I didn't want to push her. So, we took things much slower, and my only expectation was to get her confident on the ramp and swimming in the pool.

I attended a second seminar with Gulnaz Zagidullina – this time with both dogs. A few things finally clicked with Riggs and he stopped hesitating when jumping off the dock. With Tess we were still working on confidence off the ramp, but the seminar environment was great to introduce spectators and other distractions.

Then the trial!

I entered Riggs in six Splashes over two days; I was really pleased with how he did. He earned six qualifying jumps, four in Novice and two in Junior. I entered Tess in four Splashes, but treated them as Try-It sessions, only swimming and jumping off the ramp. My goal with both dogs was to get them to "compete" at the trial as well as they did in practice. As far as that went – mission accomplished!

Why am I telling you this?

So that you can see how quickly you may see results with your dog. Over the period of three weeks Riggs was able to compete at his first trial, showing you what can be possible. While Tess better demonstrates, what a slower more thoughtful process might look like.

While both of my dogs are comfortable swimming and retrieving in a natural environment, with a few great tips and advice both saw tremendous improvement over a very short period. It's certainly doable with the right instruction and mindset for introducing the sport to your dog.

So, how can you repeat our success, while avoiding the pitfalls?

Three Real World Strategies To Introduce Your Dog To Dock Diving

Now, we get to the heart of the training! How do we actually teach our dog to dock dive from square one? In this book I've broken down this process into three main steps. First, we clearly need to get our dog introduced to water and comfortable swimming. For our purposes, we are going to focus on getting started in a natural body of water. Second, once our dog is comfortable with a natural body of water, we need to get them introduced to the pool environment. Finally, we need to get them comfortable jumping off the dock and ready to compete.

Introducing Your Dog To Water

There are four key steps to successfully introducing your dog to water, so here's what you can expect to learn so you can make this the most positive experience for your dog, and get them hooked on this amazing sport!

First, we're going to help you find the right body of water to introduce your dog to the water. Next, we'll cover how you can help your dog avoid injury. Third, we have to actually get your dog in the water! And lastly, we need to start introducing the necessary skills that will transfer to the dock when we move to the pool.

How to find the right natural body of water to start your dog

In this book we're going to assume your dog has never seen water, so we're approaching this as starting right at the beginning with introducing them to water. So, how are you going to introduce them? First, you need to find water!

I like to start with a natural body of water, so a pond, river, lake, or the ocean. The reason I would recommend starting in a natural environment is twofold. First, it is just going to be a whole lot more cost effective to use a natural body of water vs. a pool. Obviously, there are a lot of expenses that go into running and owning a dock diving pool, and of course they have to cover those cost somehow. So, it's quite expensive to rent a pool even for quite a short period of time, which is understandable.

Secondly, if you do rent a pool your rental time constraint is always going to be on your mind. No matter how much you tell yourself not to rush, subconsciously you'll always have a clock running in the back of your mind putting pressure on yourself.

For those reasons, I'm going to recommend starting in a natural environment. While I wish I could just tell you go to "fill in the blank" lake. However, I clearly don't know where you live so instead, I'm going to tell you what I would look for when you're looking for a natural body of water to start in.

So, what should you look for?

Shallow Water

For your dog's first visit to water, we don't need (or necessarily want) really deep water. Water up to your dog's elbow is more than sufficient for their first visit to water. Just enough that they need to pluck up the courage to get into this new wet substance. Not so deep that you have to worry about them needing to swim.

You shouldn't expect them to swim on their first visit. You just want them to go put their paws in. If you can get them to retrieve a toy, that's great. Or play near the water, but you really want to make it as low key as possible for this first visit. Eventually, you will need to find deeper water so that they actually have to swim, but it isn't necessary for your first visit or two.

© Megan Ritchie

© Megan Ritchie

Above are a few examples of natural bodies of shallow water to introduce your dog to water for the first time.

If you have a retriever, or any water-loving breed, it's probably going to be pretty easy for you. You're just going to walk along the shoreline, and they're probably going to be in the water within ten to thirty seconds. It's not going to take them long to be interested and start splashing around. However, this book wouldn't be very helpful to you if I didn't show you what else might be needed if you don't have a dog like that.

Gentle Decline

The next things you should look for in that natural environment is a gentle decline on shore and into the water. What do I mean by that?

Look for a shore that has a gentle slope on the land, and then into the water. You really want to avoid a steep bank on shore where you're forcing your dog to take a leap of faith into the water. That's going to add unnecessary stress for a more nervous dog, so let's make it as stress free as possible for them.

Just as important, look for a body of water that has that same gentle slope in the water. Many of my local lakes were man made dams, so they do have a steeper slope to hold the water, which is not ideal.

Why is a steep slope bad?

Well, for a more nervous dog (like Tess) that sudden drop off could easily scare them, especially if they can't see the ground. If they unexpectedly lose the ground under them, lose their footing, or are surprised into swimming, that's not going to be a positive experience for them. They like to have more control, and decide for themselves when to swim, and get confidence on their own timeline. Give them the time to do that.

See the photo below to see what you're looking to avoid on your first few visits. Eventually, these can be great to encourage jumping from shore, but save these for when your dog has more confidence in the water.

© Megan Ritchie

And finally, below an example of my favorite lake. You can see this particular part of the lake has a gentle decline, very consistent slope, and no sudden drops.

© Megan Ritchie

Warm Water

You are going to have some limitations depending on where you live, and what time of year you decide to start training, but if you can find warm water that's going to help at lot in making it a positive experience.

Shallower water is going to warm up faster than deeper water so that's another reason to start with shallower water. If you live in a warmer climate, warm water might be easier to find but here in Alberta most of the lakes are in the mountains so it can be late spring before all the ice has melted; and they're certainly not warm at that point.

If you have a dog that's a little thinner skinned or tends to get cold, you can always look at something like a neoprene vest. That will help them retain their body heat once they do get in and start swimming more.

Finding warm water can be a challenge, but if you're introducing them to water for the first time please do at least wait for the ice to melt. For a first swimming experience that can be quite jarring.

Keep them warm, keep them happy, keep their muscles and joint from seizing up. Every little thing you can do to make this positive is going to help long term.

Slow Moving Water

If you are considering a stream or a river, try to avoid one that has fast-moving water or rapids. Slower moving water is good, and avoid protruding boulders if possible. Again, you want them to be comfortable in the water so something fairly slow or stagnant is going to give them the best confidence boost when just learning.

© Megan Ritchie

You can see in the above photo that towards the opposite bank the water is moving with a fairly strong current, but the near shoreline is shallow enough and slow. This particular stream might be better once your dog is more confident and swimming in that more stagnant water.

Natural Hazards

It likely goes without saying, but you'll also want to avoid bodies of water that have a lot of natural hazards. Alligators and Crocodiles aren't a concern in Alberta, but if you live in an area where those types of dangers are something you have to consider, choose your practice area wisely! You'll also want to avoid an environment with a lot of branches, logs, or obstacles in the water that your dog could get caught in and be unable to escape; punctures from those protruding hazards is also a concern. Usually, this just means moving down the shoreline a little bit; but one of our local man made lakes has a field of tree stumps underwater. So, knowing that you certainly wouldn't want your dog to jump into that and injure themselves.

Another consideration is certainly the "health" of that water, we've all heard news stories of dogs getting sick after playing in, or drinking, unhealthy water. This can take many forms, locally certain algae growth is very deadly to dogs, and rain runoff carrying with it motor oil, pesticides, and other chemicals can be a concern.

If you know of issues (like algae, and parasites) with certain health impacts on pets, avoid those bodies of water. Check for government websites in your area and see if you can find a listing of affected lakes and water ways. You can also ask your veterinarian about local concerns; most are well aware of local areas to avoid. As an added safety precaution, bath or rinse your dog after every swim.

While the ocean can be a very good place to teach your dog to swim, salt water definitely brings its own risks. For splashing and swimming salt water isn't usually an issue, but once you start playing with toys you really need to watch how much salt water your dog swallows.

© Megan Ritchie

Excessive salt-water ingestion can cause seizures, kidney injury, and severe dehydration; so be mindful of how much water they are drinking as they pick up their toys. Bring fresh water for them if they need a drink. You'd be surprised how quickly salt water poisoning can happen. If you are worried your dog has too much salt water in their system, take them to the veterinarian immediately.

How to avoid injury

When starting any new sport our goal usually includes improved health for our dog, and ourselves, so we certainly want to avoid injuring or harming them through our training. Let's walk through some actions you can take to reduce the chance of injury to your dog.

Safe Shoreline

This likely goes without saying, but look for a clean area with no garbage or debris. As frustrating as it is, it isn't uncommon to find broken bottles, glass, random car parts, twine, left over picnic trash, and other garbage in these natural areas.

Please be careful and scan your playing area for dangers from human garbage…and of course if you can help and pick up some of that debris all the better for your next visit.

Footing

Good footing is an important thing to watch for in your natural body of water. If you have access to a sandy beach that's fantastic! Rocks can be okay, but smaller and more worn rocks are better. Near Calgary most of our local water bodies have quite rounded river rock. Which works well. It

depends a little on the size of your dog and how tough their pads are.

If the rocks are larger and you have a smaller dog, you might be worried about your dog tripping on rocks or getting their foot stuck between rocks and injuring themselves. If they seem confident with the footing, and you feel it's safe then go ahead and practice there. However, watch out for bigger or jagged rocks.

My dogs are pretty big, but one of rivers nearby is a great example of "bad" footing for dock diving practice. The rocks have been built up around the left bank of the river to stop erosion.

They're probably more than a foot in diameter and very square and rough. To me, that's just too easy to get a foot stuck in between the rocks. If they jump at the wrong time it's very easy to injure a leg or pad. So, definitely watch out for that.

© Megan Ritchie

More ocean specific, but barnacles can be a big problem for our dogs. Again, I learnt this one the hard way, and I hope you can learn from my mistakes.

I had Tess out at the ocean as a young dog, this particular beach had rocks and footing that normally I'd be quite happy with, however, there were barnacles on all over the beach. Tess was just playing on the beach, we weren't dock diving or playing with toys, but another dog came up to her they started playing. They were both running around, having a lot of fun and I didn't think twice about it.

© Megan Ritchie

I got back to the house after our play session and her paws seemed sore. When I examined them, the underside of her pads were all ripped up, parts of them were bleeding – but largely just torn up and tender. So again, please be aware of the footing when playing at the ocean.

© Megan Ritchie

Seaweed and algae growth can also be a concern, especially if they coat the rocks or shoreline making it slippery. If the footing is slippery it can easily cause your dog to lose their footing, making it a potentially negative experience for a newer swimmer, or torn muscles for your more experienced swimmer.

However, usually this is more of a danger to us humans who lose our footing and get hurt, than our dogs, but it certainly can affect them too. Algae and seaweed can also cover other dangers like broken glass, so proceed with caution.

Drowning

I think we would all agree that the risk of drowning and death would qualify as an injury, and one that we definitely want to avoid! So, let's talk doggie life jackets and when to use them.

The easy answer – whenever you feel it's necessary!

The longer answer? If you have a breed that is thought to be ill-suited for swimming; if they have short muzzles, are prone to difficulty breathing, or have a stockier build that makes swimming harder, it might be something to consider no matter how much they love the water.

A more contentious opinion, I would suggest that any dog should wear a life jacket the first time they swim. Is it necessary for breeds that are natural swimmers?

No probably not, but it will give you peace of mind. It helps them keep their back level as they learn what position their body should be in to swim.

Conversely, it's been argued that life jackets encourage dogs to never learn how to swim properly since they are always supported. I don't know what the truth is, but I feel more comfortable with a life jacket on my dogs, so that's what I do.

If your pup gets in water that's too fast or deep for them, if they panic, if you're not able to get to them fast enough, the life jacket buys time.

Also, if you are required by law to have your dog on leash, you might prefer to hook it up to a life jacket instead of a collar. The life jacket will give you more ability to pull them back to shore if you need to, it will also keep the leash up and out of the water, and keep you in compliance with bylaw officers!

Since I mentioned leash use, I have seen many people online suggest using a leash or rope (in the pool or at the lake) to guide the dog if needed, and to pull them out of rapids or danger if necessary. I personally get a little leery about using a leash or rope, especially in a natural environment, primarily because you don't always know what's under the surface of the water and what the leash might get caught on.

A loose leash or rope, that's floating along behind your dog could get caught on many natural obstacles like: sticks, logs, garbage, or anything else under the water that you can't see. It can also get tangled in your dog's legs. So, my personal preference is not to use a leash especially in a natural environment, but if I had to, I probably would hook up a retractable leash to the life jacket.

I'm usually not a big fan of retractable leashes, but this is an exception where I think it provides more benefit than a traditional six-foot leash. If you use a retractable leash, you're not going to need to worry about getting tangled in the leash yourself, about keeping the unfed line organized, all while allowing your dog room to swim and play with more freedom. Most of the time the dog will be downhill of you when they are in the water, so if the retractable leash is clipped to their life jacket it will be easier for you to keep the line out of the water and decrease the chance of it getting tangled on natural obstacles.

For safety, if I was to attach any leash to my dogs while they are swimming in a natural environment, I would carry a knife on me. In the event of an emergency where the leash gets caught on an obstacle and is risking my dogs' life, I would need that knife to be able to quickly free my dog from being trapped and potentially drowned. Rivers and rapids might be a higher risk area, but I would recommend you have it in case of an emergency regardless of where you are practicing.

However, it is understandable that you may choose to use a leash or rope so you can safely guide your dog out of the water or away from danger, especially if you are unable to enter the water yourself. You need to weigh the risks and benefits and decide what is best for you and your dog.

Cold Water Shock And Hypothermia

As previously mentioned, a lot of local lakes are very, very cold even throughout the summer. If that's the case in your area as well, you're definitely running a risk of shock if you plunge your dog into cold water repeatedly, best case scenario it causes muscle seizing and shock, and in the worst-case prolonged swimming can cause hypothermia.

Some breeds might be a little hardier for cold water, since they were bred to work in it, but if you have a breed that's a little bit more sensitive to cold weather or water you might need to be more careful. First, it might not be a positive experience for them, but second, you're risking muscle seizing and cold water shock.

If you've ever jumped in a cold lake and experienced the shock and your loss of breath, you know what your dog is experiencing.

If you know your dog is more susceptible due to their breed or age, make sure to dry them off and warm them up quickly after you're done playing. If you see that are shaking and shivering while playing that can mean they're at risk for hypothermia, so definitely dry them off and get them in the car to warm them up.

If you're limited to cold-water environments and you're doing a lot of training in that cold water, a neoprene vest might be ideal to make sure your dog stays safe and has fun. A neoprene vest will help keep those muscles and body warm, and reduce the risk of shock allowing your dog to play longer.

Introducing Your Dog To Water

Now that you've found a great natural body of water to play in, and you know how to reduce the risk of injury, it's time to actually introduce them to the water.

Let's get started!

Walking Along The Shore

For a very low stress introduction, you've found a shallow, gentle grade, body of water ahead of time. Now all you're going to do is walk along the shoreline, or stand near the water - and basically ignore the water. Really just let the dog discover it themselves. If you ignore the water, within about ten seconds your dog is going to start to check it out themselves, put a toe in, sniff it, drink the water, or splash around. If they go in of their own volition, you can certainly encourage them for showing confidence and going in, but more or less ignore anything they do before they go into the water. Show them it's no big deal and let them discover it on their own.

© Megan Ritchie

Most dogs probably aren't going to need a whole lot of encouragement to go in. If you're drawn to dock diving you probably have a breed that has some sort of affinity to water, or even better you already know that your dog likes water. That's really all there is to the introduction, just play and walk near the shore.

What do I do if they don't go in on their own?

You can jazz them up playing next to the water. You can walk a few feet into the water and again, just walk along the shoreline staying in the shallow water. Usually, if you're in the water that's going to give them the confidence to go in themselves, or they'll feel just a little bit of stress and want to join you. Giving them that last push to pluck up the courage to come in and visit with you. Without unnecessarily complicating things, that's likely going to be enough to get them in.

If you're really struggling and neither of those are working, to the best of your ability use your dog's biggest internal motivator. If your dog is really motivated by people, try walking a little bit further out into the water, or have their favorite family member's go out a little deeper and try to play a recall game with one of you in the water and one on shore. Rewarding your dog for being brave and going to visit their favorite person in the water.

Alternatively, you can encourage them with a toy. If they're very toy driven, throw their favorite floating toy a couple inches into the water, encourage them to go pick it up, and reward them when they bring it back with a couple throws on the shore. Then try another throw into the water, this time a couple inches further in. That way we can slowly build their confidence to go further and further out into the water.

A toy is a great choice if your dog is toy motivated, but what if they're not toy or person motivated? Or what if it isn't working in this environment? Sometimes our dogs are just nervous enough that they're not interested in their favorite toy right now. In that case, I'd try to encourage them to come into the water using food to lure them in.

To use the luring technique again I would stand in the water a foot or so in, just enough that your dog would get their paws wet; show your dog a treat and encourage them to come get it.

If they are really stressed, you may have to reward them just for standing on the shoreline (with no paws in the water), or even reward them just for looking at the water. If they look at the water, use your marker word (like "yes" or "good"), say yes when they look at the water, then give them a treat right away.

Once they're confident with that, wait until they get their tip toe or nail in the water, then say "yes" and give them a treat. Then ask for a little more, using treats in your hand you can slowly lure then into the water, once they get in a little further say yes, and give them a treat.

To recap, if your dog is struggling with getting into the water, those are the three techniques you can use: toys, people, or luring with treats.

For 95% of you you're never going to have to use this, but if you do find you're in a bit of a bind, if your dog's not going into the water.

Those are definitely three strategies you can use. For the majority of you, you're simply going to open the car door, let them see the water, and they're probably going to be in the water before you know it. However, if you are having trouble those are three techniques to try.

Regardless of which technique you use, you want to gradually increase the distance and difficulty, but don't forget to include some easier confidence boosting throws or recalls as well. If you're asking them to go in the water, don't go from asking them to get their toes wet to throwing the ball thirty feet into the water and asking them swim and get it.

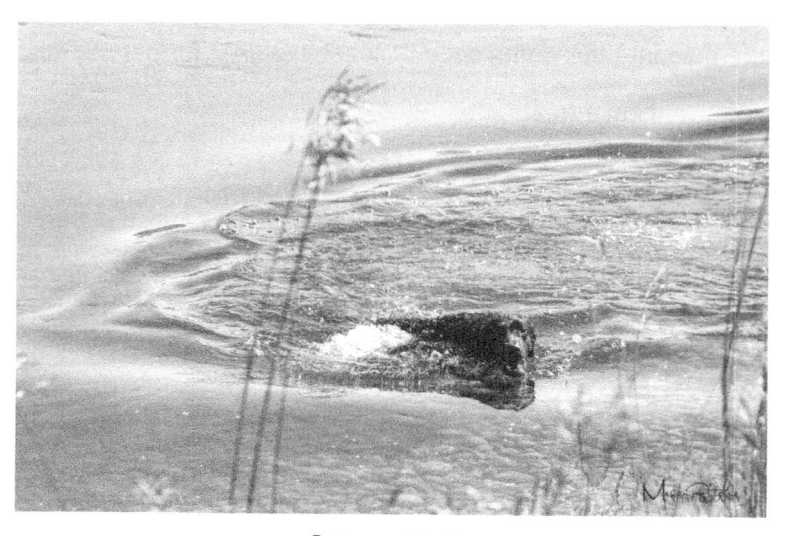

© Megan Ritchie

That's too big of a jump in difficulty level. Some dogs probably can do it, and some are naturally going to be more likely to be successful, but other dogs are going to need a little bit more help in between those two steps.

Instead try throwing a ball an inch into the water, and then throw two catches on the shore, then throw the ball two feet into the water, and then one on shore, and then five feet into the water. If they're confident with that, maybe they're even swimming a little bit, then you can throw it the ball five feet out for ten throws, and then maybe you need a confidence boosting throw that's only two feet into the water. Then you can push them with a ten-foot throw into the water.

Just keep mixing things up, throw some that stretch their confidence and ability, and some that are more confidence building. Nothing will kill their motivation and drive more than constantly pushing them with harder and harder retrieves.

If your dog is not going in for toys at this point, you can do the same thing with people or treats. If you're using people, that probably means you have to wade out. If you and a family member are using recall games from the shore to the water, you're going to vary how deep you are wading into the water – and therefore how far the dog has to wade out to get to you.

However, you want to encourage your dog to start going in after a toy, because ultimately at a competition you can't be in the water.

Building The Foundations For The Dock

Now that your dog is confidently going into the water and swimming from a gradual decline, we need to start to introduce the skills that they will need to move to the dock (and remain stress free).

What would lack of confidence look like?

Hesitation to go into the water would be the biggest indicator. If you're still luring them into the water with food, or using people, they likely aren't there just yet. If you're using toys but they aren't rushing in to get them.

If they love the toy when you throw it on shore, but whine or hesitate to jump in and get it from the water – they aren't there yet. Just keep working away increasing their confidence.

Ideally, I want to open the car door and have them rush into the water, with or without a toy.

If they're not at that point, just keep encouraging them. Keep it lighthearted and don't put too much pressure on them. 90% of dogs will work through these steps really quickly – like in a ten-minute session their first day at the water. Some of you are probably reading this and going, "Oh my goodness, this is so simple!"

For 90% of you, that's going to be the case, but for the 10% of you that are struggling I wanted to cover it so you know how to deal with those issues.

If you've determined your dog is confident and you're starting to think about moving to the dock, now what?

Introducing The Jump

One of the first things you can try is to increase the grade of the shore (and the entrance into the water). Now, you are looking for a steeper bank where you can start to encourage them to push off from a steep bank and actually jump into the water.

© Megan Ritchie

A location like above is a good choice, it's a fairly even decline, but steeper than we've used to date. The water they would jump into is actually fairly deep, so they aren't going to get injured if they jump into the water.

This is something Tess really struggles with, she really doesn't like that sudden drop off, especially if it happens under the water and she loses her footing unexpectedly.

That's a similar issue your dog might experience when you move to the pool. So, you want to introduce it in the natural environment so you can start to build their confidence with this new skill and challenge.

Increasing the grade adds that degree of difficulty, and is a great example of where a life jacket can help. For one thing it's buoyancy in general will help because even if they simply walk into the water, they don't have to make that decision to leap into the water to swim, the life jacket is just going to gently lift them off their feet, and before they know it, they're swimming. As you increase the difficulty on your dog, watch your dog's comfort level.

Increasing Confidence In the Jump

If your dog starts acting hesitant to jump in the water as you increase the grade on shore, maybe you've pushed them too far, too fast. However, a little bit of hesitation is okay, as you increase the difficulty. You have to judge your own dog's sensitivity to change. I know I could probably ask my younger dog Riggs to jump off a vertical cliff and he would jump in, but Tess is going to take a more thoughtful approach to build her confidence as the incline of the shore increases.

If you're seeing a little bit of hesitation and uncertainty as you increase the difficulty that's normal, but you don't want them stressing at the shore for a long time. You're going to use that same observation and skill when you move to the dock, but one or two seconds of being like "Oh, I'm not sure. I'm not sure. Fine, I'll jump in and do it." That's okay.

So, you are looking at their confidence in launching into the water, and pushing off into a swim if there is a sudden drop under water.

At this point, if they're confident and you know they're having fun because they're willingly jumping into the water and swimming, that's a great time to introduce your dog to their future dock diving toys.

Introducing Dock Diving Toys

When you first introduce your dog to the water, you're going to use whatever floating toy you need to encourage them to get in the water. Most of us start our dogs using regular floating tennis balls or sticks, and while they are effective as swimming toys, they aren't ideal for dock diving.

© Megan Ritchie

Something, I hadn't really considered prior to the seminars I attended, but Gulnaz mentioned in the podcast, tennis balls (especially the rubber ones) can be really slippery for dogs in the water.

The orange Chuckit! Ultra Ball's are very popular as water toys, they are relatively inexpensive, generally float well, and are easy to see. However, your dog can puncture them which results in them losing their ability to float – so be careful where and when you use them if you can't call your dog off the toy if it sinks. However, something I'd seen but didn't really clue into until talking with Gulnaz was how slippery they are. I was watching Tess in the pool trying to grab one, and it was like watching her bob for apples. She'd try to bite it, but it'd slip away. So, they aren't ideal for dock diving use, since you want our dog to quickly and accurately bite the toy and swim out. However, for an introduction to water you need to work with what motivates your dog.

Now that your dog is more confident in the water you can start to introduce new toys and build drive for specific dock diving toys, rather than only using what your dog likes best.

We'll go over some of the toys a little bit later, but briefly your dock diving toys might include: bumpers, floating discs, or Kong Wubba's. Basically, any floating toy that you can throw easily and consistently. Everybody's dog is going to be a little bit different. If you're very comfortable throwing a disc, a disc can be a good choice.

However, if you're not good at throwing a disc, a disc would not be a good choice. If you're throwing in really windy conditions, you might want to look for a heavier toy. The more balanced the toy the easier it's going to be for you to throw consistently.

A plastic hunting style bumper is a good toy for medium sized dogs, it's durable for repeated play sessions. Heavy enough to throw in windy conditions, and it floats high in the water so it's easy for your dog to see.

A lighter bumper like the Chuckit! Amphibious Bumper is very similar, but it's going to get pushed around in the wind a little more. It has a soft but durable bite zone, which encourages a newer dog to pick it up – compared to a harder plastic bumper.

As important as it is to find a toy your dog likes, you need to find a toy you can throw consistently. This is where the balance of the toy becomes very important.

When it comes to your dog actually jumping off the dock, you want to be able to throw the toy just in front of where your dog lands. For example, if your dog can jump ten feet off the dock (or shore), you're going to want to have your toy land at least five feet in front of that – so fifteen feet from the dock edge.

Before you move to the pool, you'll want to start to introduce these new toys. When you move to the new environment you don't want to surprise them with another new thing, and introduce new toys. You also don't want to waste your pool time (and money) experimenting with new toys. Far better to practice with them and build drive when you don't have that time crunch in the back of your mind.

Introducing Your Dog To The Dock

Now that your dog is confident in the water, they are confidently jumping into the water in a natural environment, and they love their new dock diving toys, you're ready to move to the pool.

The first thing you need to do is find a dock!

For this book we are focusing on North America Diving Dogs (NADD) because it is the most recognized association, and its titles are recognized by the American Kennel Club and Canadian Kennel Club. However, if you prefer a different dock diving organization the process would work the same way. To learn more about the different associations, check out the association list at the end of this book.

To find a local dock near you, I would recommend two methods: (1) check out the approved pools through the NADD events page, or (2) do a Google search for a dock diving pool near you.

If you visit the NADD events page, you can search by location, and it will pull up any upcoming events. You do not have to sign up for an event or competition at this point, you just want to know what the closest pool is. You might have to expand the dates in the search function to find all the local pools.

Now that you've found a local pool, you can visit their website and see what services they offer. If they offer private lessons, classes, or seminars you've hit the jackpot! If it is available, I would definitely recommend you get instruction and real-time feedback, but if all that's available is pool rental time, this book will help you get started without further instruction. If you are able to get some instruction from a trainer, this book will give you an idea of what you can expect in those early sessions.

Once you've booked some pool time, grab a few of your dog's favorite floating toys, their life jacket, and hit the pool!

A Positive Introduction To The Pool

When you arrive at the pool, you're actually going to take your dog to the ramp (attached to the dock) and not the dock itself. The actual dock is usually raised two feet above the surface of the water, which is usually nerve wracking for the dog's first jump in the pool.

Any sanctioned dock diving pool will have a forty-foot dock which is used in competition, usually the dock has an AstroTurf surface or carpet to allow the dog to get a good grip when they are running and jumping off the dock. Right next to the dock, there will be a ramp that leads into the water.

The ramp is the best place to start for a few reasons; first, as I mentioned it helps to build your dog's confidence and acts as a good middle step before heading to the dock itself. Second, and perhaps most importantly your dog needs to know how to safely exit the pool once they do jump in. By starting at the ramp, you are teaching your dog where they need to go to get out of the pool.

Ramp Work

Upon arrival at the pool take your dog down to the ramp with a couple toys. You already know your dog loves and is confident in water, now you have to show them that the water in the pool is exactly the same as their favorite place to practice. To start, you're going to do a very similar routine to how you started your dog in water. I would highly recommend you put a life jacket on your dog for their first time in the pool.

© Megan Ritchie

Most facilities have life jackets available to use or rent, if you don't own one – or think your dog won't need it for long.

The life jacket is important for a few reasons, while it certainly will help them swim that actually isn't the primary reason to put it on. At this point, if you've done the other training your dog can already swim, so that's not what the life jacket is primarily for - though it will help if they need additional support. The primary reason we want the life jacket for the introduction to the pool is so we can guide your dog in the water if needed.

So, take your dog to the ramp with their favorite toy, and simply throw it an inch or two into the water. Or, even just roll the toy down the ramp. The toy is going to splash into the water, and with any luck your dog will run down the ramp, grab the toy, and bring it back.

If your dog is confident going to retrieve the toy from the bottom of the ramp, you're going to alternate some further throws, and then some confidence building throws. It might go something like this:

- Two inches into the water, dog can still touch the ramp
- Two feet into the water directly in front of the ramp
- Three inches into the water
- Two feet into the water
- One foot into the water
- Four feet into the water
- Two feet into the water
- Six feet into the water
- Three feet into the water
- Eight feet into the water
- Four feet into the water

At this point all the throws are still directly in front of you, so the dog can walk then swim into the water. If your dog is showing confidence and starts jumping from the ramp into the water (rather than walk or run out then start swimming) you're ready to move onto the next step.

© Mahalia Goodey, Prairie Echo Photography

Your dog might hesitate when they have to transition from walking out and picking up the toy to actually needing to swim to pick up the toy. This point is going to be different for every dog depending on their size.

A Jack Russell is going to have to start swimming a lot closer to the ramp than a Great Dane. It's very common for dogs to hesitate a bit when they first have to swim – even if they love swimming! So, don't be surprised if your dog is a little unsure.

If your dog does start hesitating you want to encourage them when they show small signs of bravery, that might be stretching to reach the toy (even if they don't swim), that might be pawing with a front paw, any movement or interest in moving towards the toy we want to reward. When your dog is successful and either swims or pick up the toy, you want to give them a lot of praise, then include a few easy reward throws to jazz them up and reward them for their courage.

Every dog is going to move at their own speed, some dogs like my younger dog Riggs who are more confident are going to be able to do this in a couple throws their first session in the pool. Other more nervous dogs like my older dog Tess need a little more time to get comfortable. Don't try to rush this process! It takes as long as it takes, the more pressure you put on your dog the more they are going to get worried about the process and the slower your progress. So, treat your first session like a day at the beach, take it easy and enjoy the process.

At no point are we going to push or pull the dog into the water. That isn't going to leave a positive impression on them and will make them much less likely to want to participate in this sport. Never fear, they will learn to love the pool if you keep at it.

Just to give you an example, Riggs was comfortable on the ramp and ready for the dock during his first ten minutes at the pool, Tess has had four sessions in the pool and still isn't quite comfortable to move to the dock. However, she is having a lot of success on the ramp. While each dog is going to progress at a different rate, you will see a lot of success very quickly from your ramp work – even if they aren't on the dock yet.

If your dog is starting to jump off the ramp into the water, you should be thinking they might be ready to try the dock. Before you move to the dock, you want to try one more thing first. So far, we've been throwing along the same path as the ramp, but now we are going to throw the toy at a 90-degree angle off the ramp into the center of the pool. This might be somewhere around the 10-15-foot mark on the pool. We want to see if the dog is confident jumping off the ramp into the water itself. Since the ramp has an edge, they will lose their footing if they try to step or swim off the ramp at that 90-degree angle.

© Megan Ritchie

If your dog does well with the jump off the ramp into the middle of the pool, it's time to move to the dock!

Where's The Exit

As previously mentioned, one of the primary reasons to do the ramp work is to teach your dog how to safely get out of the pool. It might seem obvious to us how to get in and out, but a lot of dogs can panic when they get into the pool and aren't sure how to get out. Many will try to climb the walls of the pool, the fencing around the pool, or even try to climb back up onto the dock itself. Many will panic a little bit if they aren't sure where to go. Sound travels a little differently in the water, and dogs can have a hard time identifying where you are calling them from in their distressed state.

The ramp work helps your dog learn where the exit is. This is another reason it's recommended that you use a life jacket on your dog. The handle of the life jacket will give you - or an instructor - something to grab onto to help guide your dog back to the ramp and safely exit the pool.

Since it can stress dogs out if they don't know how to get out, many will lose their proper swimming form, their bum sinks, they start splashing more, causing them more distress. This is another great reason to leave on the life jacket until they are more comfortable in the pool setting. It's a little like you thinking to breathe. Most of the time you really don't have to think about it, your body just knows what to do, but if you go for a run and are out of breath, or get startled and gasp for air, all of a sudden, you're definitely aware of your breathing. I think it's the same for our dogs. They can swim, but in a new environment while trying to figure out a new sport, sometimes they lose a little of those skills until they become more comfortable in this new space.

So again, that life jacket is going to give you a way to guide your dog out of the pool if necessary, or simply just give them added buoyancy to give them those few extra seconds to orient themselves, and figure out where they need to go next. This is typically a temporary measure until we are sure they are confident and can get out of the water on their own. Of course, if you want to use it forever you can continue to use it and they can even compete with it on.

Get Ready To Get Wet

While the sport is intended to get your dog into the pool, there is a very good chance that you're going to get a little wet on your first visit to the pool as well. Whether that's going in with your dog for a swim (if they need a little more support – and the pool allows it), or even just going in up to your knees on the ramp to help pull them back onto the ramp if they have trouble getting out of the water, or to retrieve one of their toys.

© Megan Ritchie

Give Me Heat!

Keeping with our theme of keeping this experience positive for your dog, warm weather and warm water will definitely help! Not a lot of pools are heated, but it's definitely a bonus if it is. Of course, warm weather helps too. If you're in a warm climate, it's going to be a lot nicer for them to jump into cool water.

In Calgary, the first dock diving event of the year is held in April at an outdoor venue, and it almost always snows that weekend. It's definitely not the nicest introduction to dock diving when it is snowing outside, and they are jumping into freezing cold water. So, that's just something to keep in mind when planning your first swim session.

Don't Forget The Toys

I touched on this a little bit already, but be sure to bring their favorite toy, and even better a variety of toys. Dock diving specific toys are better for long term training, but for your first few times at the pool bring whatever it takes to entice them to jump into the water.

Sometimes toys that work great in a natural environment aren't enough to encourage them to play in the pool, sometimes you need to bring out the "big guns". So, the more toys you can bring the better until you know what really motivates them.

If your dog is really struggling, sometimes just having a new and novel toy will help. If you've ever brought home a new toy for your dog in a shopping bag only to have your dog riffle through the bag to try to get their new toy, then you know the allure of a new toy to your dog. Another technique that can work is bringing another dog's toy. If you've set up a training session and are going with a friend. Try using one of their dog's toys. Sometimes a stolen toy is more fun than playing with your own – even if they're identical.

No Expectations

Something I've heard a lot from others starting in dock diving, and caught myself thinking, is "Oh, my dog loves the water. They love to play. They love to swim. You know, this is going to be no problem." You're already going in with high expectations that our dogs are going to catch on super quickly, and be jumping off the dock in the first ten minutes.

While for some dogs that is possible, it's the exception not the rule. If you go in with no expectations, I can all but guarantee you're going to come away blown away with their progress, but as much as possible try not to put a lot of pressure and expectations on them.

This is easier said than done if you're renting the pool or attending a trial for your dog's first pool exposure, and you're feeling time pressure. Maybe you've only rented the pool for half an hour, or you have a three-minute Try-It Splash at a trial; with those time limits it's easy to feel that time pressure. Which sets you up to try to make things happen faster than might be best for your dog.

Like I said, with my older dog Tess (at the time I'm writing this) we've been playing on the ramp for four weeks, she likes to swim and jump into the water in a natural environment, but she's not ready to jump off the dock yet. She's starting to get more confident jumping 90 degrees off the ramp into the pool, and that progress is ok. As long as we keep these practices positive, I have no doubt she will eventually jump off the dock, but if I put a lot of pressure on her, it might never happen. Some dogs are going to be more sensitive than others, and you really need to know your dog's personality to know how hard to push. If in doubt, err on the side of taking things slowly.

© Mahalia Goodey, Prairie Echo Photography

Find The Best Learning Environment

There are a lot of new things to adjust to in the trial environment, they have to get used to the pool itself, noise, spectators, judges, other dogs, your nerves, a photographer snapping away. It's a lot to take in when trying to learn something new, you'd never set out to learn a new language in the middle of a busy street with a teacher yelling words for you to repeat over the din of passing cars – why? You know it would be a terrible environment to try to learn something new, but we expect this from our dogs all the time.

So, try not to start them in the pool during a trial if you can avoid it. Sometimes you don't have much choice, if a mobile dock at a trial is all that you have available to you nearby, but if you can attend a seminar or rent the pool prior to a trial that's a much better learning environment for your dog.

If you compete in other sports with your dog, and they are already used to a trial environment, they may be more resilient to learning in that environment. You're still going to feel the pressure of the time limit, so it still isn't ideal, but you can make it work if that's all that's available.

If you've never attended a trial in any sport, a trial environment is going to be a hard place to learn for both of you. People are generally very friendly and welcoming to newcomers, but it's always a challenge to figure out where you need to go, what registration you need, how to enter, what the rules are. All before you even know if you like the sport! So again, I wouldn't recommend this route. If you don't have anything close, I'd recommend making a weekend and booking some pool time as close as you can. If you really can't do that, do as much homework as you can before entering a Try-It at an NADD event.

Common Problems & Trouble Shooting

We've already addressed some training issues that can arise when teaching your dog how to dock dive, but here we'll go into more details.

My Dog Won't Go Into The Water

Just like the water in a natural environment your dog might show some hesitation to go into the water in the pool. They might love swimming at their local lake, but they're not sure this pool thing is the same.

What can you do?

Basically, the same strategy recommended for the lake. If your dog is more food motivated (and the facility allows it), you can try and lure them into the water using food. Lead them to the edge of the ramp, and give them a treat there.

Then take them to play away from the ramp for a little bit, when they're excited and engaging with you bring them back down, try and lure them into the water again. You can use hand targeting if your dog is familiar with that cue.

Simply, you're just going to slowly use food to lure them closer or deeper into the water. Usually, you don't have to build this up to actual swimming just enough to convince them they can get their feet wet. Once they are comfortable and confident going into the water to receive their treat, it's time to bring back the toys and try again.

If your dog is more people motivated you can use people instead of treats. This can be getting into the water with them, or having someone stand outside of the pool at the opposite end, and call the dog to them.

At the first seminar I attended we had a funny situation arise, there was a Labradoodle that was really struggling and afraid to go into the pool. The dog loved the water in a natural environment, but he wasn't quite sure what the heck this pool thing was.

They tried luring him with food, they tried toys, even the dogs most favorite toys in the world weren't working. Then by chance, the dog caught sight of one of the other owners at the end of the pool – who was taking pictures of their session. The dog saw the owner outside the pool, the owner called and encouraged the dog to come over. The dog did a nervous little dance at the ramps edge, then all of a sudden plunged right in and swam over to them. The dog did an awesome victory lap and loved swimming in the pool, and had no issues after that.

What was starting to look like a frustrating day half way through the seminar with "no progress" all of a sudden was a massive success. Within ten minutes that same dog was leaping off the dock and was continuing to swim his victory lap around the pool. It was so amazing to see.

If the food and people don't work, you might be able to pick your dog up and carry them into the pool. This depends on a few factors, first you're dog really has to trust you, and not hold a grudge!

If they are upset that you carried them into the pool, you're going to have a really hard time catching them next time to carry them in, or even getting them through the door to the ramp. So, use this cautiously.

If you do use it (or the instructor does), the best thing to try is to slowly carry them into the water with you, gently release them into the water to float (with their life jacket on) and encourage them to swim back to the ramp.

For some dogs that's all they need to break them out of their mental block, and they will probably become comfortable swimming after a few repetitions. If they are comfortable swimming back to the ramp, you can start to put their favorite toy between them and the ramp and encourage them to pick it up on the way back. If they appear confident with that, you can try throwing the toy and see if they will do the whole process on their own.

If you do use this method, the life jacket handle will help the person in the water guide the dog back to the ramp.

When do you *not* want to "force" your dog into the pool?

Most of the time I would not recommend this method, but if they have a mental block it can be helpful if they have the right relationship with you, and mindset...but they also need to be the right size. It would be almost impossible for me to lift my 80-pound dog into the pool if he didn't want to go. So, this technique is limited to dogs that you can easily lift. You cannot force your dog into the pool during competition, so long term this is not a good strategy, but it can be a way to break that mental block if you've tried everything else.

My Dog Isn't Playing With Their Toys

If your dog normally loves their toys and happily dives in for them at your local watering hole, but all of a sudden won't play with them at the pool try to bring your dog back to the dock or further up the ramp and engage with them there.

If they will play with their toy on the dock or ramp, try to get them amped up, then quickly move the ramp and toss the toy in the water (just enough that they have to get their feet wet).

You might have to yo-yo back and forth between the water and the dock getting them jazzed up, and then bringing that positive energy to the pool itself. Again, you're going to alternate between something easy (like playing on the dock) and something more difficult (like swimming in the water). Sometimes using a novel toy is enough to get them re-engaged with playing with you. So be prepared with a few different toys to alternate during your play session to keep their interest level high.

You can use similar techniques that we've used for dog's that aren't toy driven, so you can use people, you can use food to lure, you can also use another dog – if you have one that is further along in their training.

Right now, I'm thinking using another dog might be the strategy I use to encourage Tess to jump off the dock itself for the first time. I think it'll be less stressful for her if I use Riggs as a motivator. If she can see him confidently jumping off the dock a few times with her loose on the dock with him, I think that will give her that final little boost of confidence to take that first jump.

You'd obviously want to be sure that the two dogs get along, in my case my dogs do, so that isn't an issue. However, Riggs can be pushy and oblivious when playing and he has 30 pounds on Tess so just his size and energy can be intimidating to her... even though she's usually the boss between them. So that's just something I'll need to watch out for. If he starts pushing her around or might accidently push her in, I'll have to take him out of the picture and continue to build her confidence solo.

If your dog isn't that toy driven at home, or at the lake, they're not going to magically become toy driven at the pool. You need to build up that toy drive away from the pool before you can ask them for it at the pool.

How can you do that?

There are a few different ways you can go about it. First you can use restrained play. So, you're going to hold onto your dog's collar or life jacket, and hold them back. Try to get them excited and jazzed up, then throw a ball away from them while continuing to hold them back. Wait for them to get interested in the toy and struggling to try to get to it, then let them go.

Secondly, you can use treats. This wouldn't be my top recommendation for dock diving, if you can avoid it I would. If you use this method, you're going to use shaping to teach them to love retrieving their toy. If you bring out the toy, hide it from them in your hand, try to get them interest in it, then as soon as they look at the toy or make a move to take it from you, say your marker word (like "yes"), and give them a treat.

Next, ask for a little more, wait for them to paw it, then say "yes" and give them the treat. Then you're going to up the ante and now they are going to have to bump it with their face, you'll say "yes", and give a treat. Then they have to touch it with their mouth. Then maybe I'm going to throw it and they have to pick it up a little bit - even if they pick it up and drop it, that's okay. You'll say "yes", give him a treat. You're just going to gradually build your expectations from looking at it, to picking it up, bringing it back, all to get their treat.

That is a method you can use, but it's not a top recommendation for a really toy driven sport like dock diving. Most dog's find it challenging to go back and forth between toy rewards and food rewards. They're often more driven by one versus another. For some dogs, if you try and play with toys and then give them a treat, there's no way they're eating that treat. They're too interested in that toy.

My younger dog Riggs is that way with a tennis ball. If I show him a tennis ball, it does not matter what other toy I bring out. It does not matter what food I bring out. He will not eat it. That tennis ball is king. While for other dogs the opposite is true.

If you have a dog that's a real food hound, the second you bring out those treats they will lose and all interest in any toy that they have around them. For that reason, I don't recommend the treat method unless you've exhausted other methods.

You can also use toys to reward your dog. If you've thrown a toy for your dog and they show *any* interest whatsoever, you're going to say "yes" and throw another toy for them. Mainly you're just going to get really excited anytime they show interest in that toy, and keep the sessions really, really short and really positive. Like 30-60 seconds long. You want to leave them wanting more and begging to keep playing. That's how I'd recommend you build up toy drive.

However, a little hack that's worth trying in a pinch, is trying a new toy, or using another dog's toy. That's not going to be a long-term fix, but if you're trying to get the most out of your 15 minutes of paid pool time, it can be effective while you continue to work on the toy drive at home.

Is My Dog Ready To Move To The Dock

It's hard to believe we've spent all this time and we've really just done ramp work. I hope that gives you an idea of how important it is to put those foundational skills in place. Now, it's time to move on to what you really signed up for – the dock diving!

When you introduced the ramp you threw your toy in a straight line out from the ramp out into the water. Gradually you've built up the distance and started to move them towards jumping off the ramp into the middle of the pool.

Now that they're jumping off the ramp, it's time to try to jump off the dock. Before you move to the dock, you want to be sure your dog is confident in jumping off the side of the ramp without hesitation. You're looking for them to be jumping into the water, rather than walking in, or allowing their life jacket to float them out to the toy.

Some dogs struggle a little making that move from jumping long off the ramp to jumping off the side – where they feel that definite edge and drop off – it can be a big leap of faith.

Sometimes, you'll see them kind of stand with their toes on the edge of that ramp. They're looking out to where you've thrown their toy and you might see them kind of pawing at the water. They might whine or cry, but eventually you want them to jump in after their toy.

Once they're jumping in confidently off that ramp, it's definitely time to try the dock.

How do you ask for their first jump?

Pretty simple on your part, you're just going to head up to the dock. There are a few different methods you can use. The AKC has a really good video on how to encourage your dog to go off the dock. The first strategy you can try is the restrained retrieve. You're simply going to bring your dog to the very edge of the dock, hold onto their collar or life jacket with one hand, and throw the toy with your other hand. Continue to hold your dog back, when they are straining to be released give them a cue word to release or jump.

They will probably whine at the edge of the pool; with any luck they will jump – or fall – in after their toy. If they don't jump in right away, a helper outside the pool can tease them a little by moving the toy around in the water. While this step is likely to stress them a little bit – they want their toy after all! We don't want to let this go on forever, so if they are stressing out and not jumping in, I'd recommend fishing the toy out of the pool, and either restraining them again and throwing the toy off the dock. Or move back to the ramp for a throw or two first, then try the dock again.

The other method you can use is to throw a toy while they are in motion and ask them to jump up ("chase") and try to catch it in the air. AKC has another video on this method that you can watch to get an idea of how this looks in action.

So, those are two different ways to motivate them. However, I would recommend starting with the restraint method. Allow them to build up just a smidge of frustration (which if they are already confident) is going to give them that little extra impulsion to jump off the dock.

Just like in the natural environment, or on the ramp, you don't need to push them in. You don't need to pressure them. You're going to let them get just a little stressed and frustrated, to the point where they just jump in and get it.

If your dog jumps into the pool right away, that's awesome! Congratulations! You're well on your path to dock diving success.

© Mahalia Goodey, Prairie Echo Photography

Jumping Off The Dock With Confidence

Once your dog has successfully jumped off the dock, the next few jumps are going to be a lot easier to get! Now that you have your first taste of success, how can you trouble shoot some common problems.

How To Build Confidence On The Dock

Your dog is jumping off the dock, but are they confident and comfortable with it?

Often with the restraint method your dog will jump (or fall) into the pool before they really have a chance to think about it. They almost surprise themselves. The first thing you need to do is praise them like crazy when this happens, really encourage them when they show confidence or jump into the pool. This is a great time to get really wild, hoot, holler, cheer them on, and tell them how smart they are!

Hesitation

Once your dog is jumping into the pool one of the most common problems is hesitating at the edge of the dock before jumping in. Your dog is willing to jump into the pool, but they have a half-second or couple second delay before jumping in.

How can you prevent or solve that issue?

The restrained release is one of the best ways to prevent hesitation, it's also a good start to solving the issue if it does crop up. By holding them back just before you release the toy, it activates an opposition reflex that we can use to our advantage. You are going to continue to keep them really close to that dock edge, restrain them prior to throwing the toy, and as soon as you release them you want them thinking "I gotta get that toy!"

Sometimes that little change is all you need to get them to stop hesitating. By staying close to the dock, they still have the choice to jump off or not, but they aren't given the chance to build up stress or choose to run back and forth around the dock.

When your dog is in the air jumping, if you see your dog flailing a little as they jump or land in the water. If they aren't staying tucked in and tight, it gives you a hint that your dog might not be confident yet. They might not be showing other signs of hesitation, but they still aren't quite sure of themselves and where they need their body to be.

© Mahalia Goodey, Prairie Echo Photography

I think the best way to explain it is thinking of Olympic diving, when everything is going as planned, they are tucked in, with their bodies positioned very precisely and balanced to allow them to put their body where it needs to be to complete the complicated twists, tucks, and summersaults.

I think it's the same with our dogs. If they're jumping and their body's kind of loose, their legs aren't tucked in very nicely, and they're flailing around as they try and find the water, they just aren't that confident yet.

That could be a sign that you want to go back and do some ramp work, and it might be a sign that maybe you just need to alternate a little bit. So throw a couple tosses off the dock, then do a couple off the ramp to build up their confidence.

Expect them not to be perfectly tucked in their first few jumps, but if you've had numerous sessions and you're still seeing this issue, I'd recommend you address that potential confidence issue.

Not Retrieving Their Toy

What if your dog is jumping in the water, but they're not retrieving the toy?

If your dog isn't very toy driven this can be a pretty common problem. First, the good news, you don't have to use a toy to compete. You don't have to throw the toy, and your dog doesn't need to retrieve it to receive a qualifying jump.

Ideally, you want to use a toy because that's going to allow you to encourage them to put their body where you want. For example, if you wanted your dog to jump higher for an Air Retrieve, if your dog will follow the toy, you can start to train them to jump higher by adding a higher arc on your throw. On the other hand, if you're working on their Distance jump, you might throw that arc longer and lower.

How can you do that?

The "hack" I'd try first, is switching out different toys. Why? Sometimes your dog just isn't crazy about the toy you're using. If you have a few different options I'd try different toys out and see if you can entice them that way. I'm a lazy trainer, so that's the short cut I'd try first.

The "proper" answer is you'll have to build toy drive away from the pool first. You don't want to use your valuable (read: expensive!) pool time working on this, so start away from the pool. There are a few ways you can do this depending on the toy you're using.

Method 1: Using Tug

If you're using a toy your dog can tug with, I'd start with that. It should work with a bumper as well. First, I'd let the toy hang at your side, very slowly move it away from the dog. You want to keep the toy slow and fairly steady.

Us humans tend to get really excited and bounce the toy around a lot and move it quickly. This is going to be much harder for your dog to track, and make them less likely to be accurate when biting – this is especially true for young puppies who have a harder time tracking with their eyes and with coordination in general.

You will want to keep the toy slowly moving away from them – not towards them – in an attempt to engage that prey and chase drive. If you still have friends you can talk into helping you with your random dog training ideas (congratulations first of all, they are keepers!), have them restrain your dog while you move about 5-10 feet away. Have your helper release your dog as you call them then slowly run away from them, making sure to keep the toy by your side, in their line of sight.

If you can get your dog interested in the toy, that's awesome! If they bite the toy (or even mouth it at first) tell them "yes" (or "good dog" or whatever your marker word is) then you can throw the toy, or let them take it from you and celebrate.

If they drop it right away, try playing with two toys. When they bite or tug the first toy, say "yes" and then throw or encourage them to tug the second toy right away. Try to keep it really fun, get excited when they show interest in the toy. Keep the sessions really short – like 90 seconds tops. You want to stop while they are still interested in the toy.

Method 2: Using Throwing

If your dog is more likely to want to chase the toy (or the toy you're playing with doesn't lend itself well to tug – like tennis balls) you might want to skip right to throwing. I would play with at least two toys, especially if your dog has a tendency to not want to give their new prize up.

Again, if you have a helper that can restrain your dog that can help build that teeny bit of frustration to make them want to chase the toy more. If you're using something that you can roll or throw long and low, start there. Low so they can easily see it (don't try to fake them out), long so they have a longer time to be successful and catch the toy.

Start to encourage your dog to interact with the toy at whatever level they are at. If they are really not that interested in it, reward them just for looking at it and appearing interested. A reward at this point might just be your praise. As they get more interested, mark and reward them for picking the toy up and returning it to you (or near you). I personally like to reward with the second toy as soon as I mark the behavior I want to see.

Each dog will be a little different depending on what stage they're at. It might look something like you throwing a low long underhand throw with a tennis ball, as soon as your dog picks up the ball, say "yes" then throw your second tennis ball in the opposite direction. Then repeat!

Once your dog is interested (and enjoying) playing with the toy away from the pool, try at the lake, or the pool.

For most of you, you wouldn't have progressed to the pool if your dog wasn't showing interest at the lake or at home. So, what do you do then?

Largely the same process, if your dog normally really loves to play with that toy it's likely just the environment. So, take it back a step.

Your best bet is going to be trying to entice them to play with their toy near the pool, but not in the water. You could play with them on the dock. This can be really helpful to pump them up, build their confidence, get them re-engaged with you, and then take them to the pool really quickly for a throw...then back to the dock to play again as their reward.

If they won't engage on the dock you might need to move off the dock, but staying as close to the pool as possible; while still having them engage and play with you.

Method 3: Treats

When you compete, you're eventually going to want to play with toys, so because of that using treats (and toys) together isn't my favorite method to try first. Often dogs have a hard time switching between treats and toys, usually they have one they prefer over the other. So, it can be challenging to switch between the two.

However, if you aren't having any luck with the other methods you can use treats to get them to engage with the toy. To use this method, you would get a handful of treats, drop the dock diving toy on the floor near them. As soon as they look at it, mark that behavior (say "yes") and then give them a treat. Wait for them to look at the toy again, mark that behavior, then give them a treat. Repeat until you see that they understand what earns the treat (they usually catch on around five repetitions).

Then up the ante and make it harder, maybe they have to walk towards the toy, or nudge the toy, or pick it up. If you make that jump too difficult for them, they might quit and stop engaging with the toy at all. *When* that happens, move back a step or two and try again. Keep their sessions short, and leave them wanting more. The end goal of course is to just play with the toy, but before moving onto Method 1 or 2 mentioned previously; try to get to where you can throw that toy and your dog will run over pick it up and return it to you for their treat.

Not Reaching For Their Toy

This is an issue that is discussed very well in AKC's Chase Method video, see the resources at the end of this book for the link to that video. If your dog is jumping and retrieving the toy but they aren't really reaching for it, or following the arc of the toy – which means you aren't going to be able to use your throw to manipulate how your dog moves in their jump, you want to encourage them to start to follow the toy.

When you're first starting this is more important so we can get your dog to jump more level, and ideally land rear end first – instead of headfirst into the pool. If they dive head first they aren't going to get the distance you're looking for, it's also going to be harder on their body.

Instead we want to teach them what AKC calls the "Chase method" where you're going to encourage your dog to jump up to actually try to catch the toy, rather than have them wait for the toy to land in the water then swim over to pick it up.

Put simply we're going to encourage your dog to jump up for the toy to take it or bite it.

How do you actually do that?

If your dog will already jump up to catch a toy, try practicing that on the dock then move towards the pool and have them jump in the direction of the pool. If that works and your dog jumps into the pool – Yay! But, that's a long shot so how can you back chain that a little bit?

You can start by holding up a toy for your dog to bite and take from you. Try putting your dog in a sit stay and move a couple feet away from them. Hold the toy a couple feet above their head, and encourage them to jump to take it. You might have to wiggle the toy, and definitely use your voice to encourage them to take it. When they do, have a party and tell them how smart they are! You can throw another toy, or tug with them to reward them for a job well done!

You can progress to practicing this by placing your dog on a raised platform (about 6 inches off the ground is all that's needed) then have them jump off the platform to take it from your hand. You might have luck using a low wooden deck, sidewalk curb, planters, children's playground equipment, an agility table or Klimb – to give you a few ideas.

Once they reliably will take it from your hand, try standing beside them, with your throwing hand and toy on their near side (so they can see the toy), then throw it in the air and encourage them to catch it. At first, you want the throw to be more up than away from you. If they don't catch it the toy would land 1-2 feet in front of you. Ideally, you'll want them to jump in the air and catch the toy. Again, you can practice this off a low platform.

Try not to repeat these too often in a single session as the impact is harder on their body.

Once your dog is reliably jumping and catching the toy in the air and stretching for it, try changing the arc of your throw and see the impact it has on your dog's body movement and reach.

Then it's time to bring those skills back to the pool!

First remind them that this new skill applies to the pool too, try a few repetitions on the dock away from the pool. Once they catch on and are performing at the same standard on the dock as they did in your practice sessions, it's time to encourage them to jump off the dock and into the pool while catching the toy.

If your dog is jumping for the toy and reaching for it, but they are still being a little lazy with their back legs and not really pushing off (like my dog Riggs!), you can try using your training platform and placing a low jump beside the platform. I used an agility table, then used a jump standard with the bar set about two inches higher than the table platform.

Then repeat the same reach drills asking your dog to jump off the platform and over the jump to get the toy. This will encourage them to clear the jump bar to get the toy. If your dog likes playing disc, using a disc and a vault toss with a lot of float can also be a great way to encourage them to really push off when they jump up.

Throwing Tips

When it comes to accuracy in your throws at the pool, a majority, if not all, of your throws are going to be underhand throws. That is going to automatically give you the arc you need for either Air Retrieve training or Distance throws.

Once your dog is trained in Air Retrieve you will no longer throw the toy, rather it'll be suspended and they will have to bite and pull it off the stand. However, as you train you can use those underhand throws to get a higher arc over a shorter distance to encourage that body motion and muscle memory in your dog.

As you practice for Distance games, you will throw underhanded with a slight arc over a much longer distance.

One tip to help your dog have more success when tracking the toy and ultimately catching it (using the Chase method), is to try to keep the toy as level and predictable as possible. This is more evident when playing with the Nerf Competition Stick or a bumper style toy. Ideally, you'd want to throw the toy as level as possible, so your dog can easily track the toy and try to bite it.

© Megan Ritchie

Sometimes you see other people throwing the bumper in more of a spin, head over tail (usually thrown holding the rope or strap rather than having it balanced in their hand). The motion of this spinning throw is going to be easy for your dog to see, but it is a much larger target for them, and not as easy to bite. Don't worry about this too much when you're first starting (your throwing isn't going to be perfect), but it'll get much more important when introducing your dog to the chase method and you want them to start catching the toy in the air.

© Megan Ritchie

Increasing Motivation

The last thing you need to know is how to increase your dog's motivation once they are successfully jumping off the dock. This will certainly make it more fun for both of you, it will also encourage your dog to bring the toy back more quickly (great for Hydro Dash!), and get more distance.

Praise Your Dog

This is the one thing I see so much across all dog sports, but praising and encouraging your dog is one of those things that's so easy to do, yet so detrimental to your training if you don't. The more encouragement you give them, and the more you tell them how happy you are with them, the more confident they're going to be doing it. Your dog has no idea what the heck this new game is, or what you're trying to get them to do. So often, when we train, we're really playing a game of "Hot and Cold" with them. The more encouragement you can give your dog when they are "getting warm" and doing what you want the more likely they're going to want to that again. So, definitely praise your dog. Reward them when they return their toy to you - especially if they're not a super toy motivated dog.

Reward Your Dog

Along with praise there are many forms of "reward" for our dogs. For many of our dogs, the chance to keep playing is a *huge* reward, so is the chance to play with their toy. When they do something you're super happy with, reward them with a tug session when they do it. Or throw a second toy for them on the dock as a reward for being super awesome.

Restrained Retrieve

In previous sections, I covered this quite a bit so I will just briefly mention it again here.

The restrained retrieve is a great way to increase motivation to jump and fetch the toy. It uses your dog's natural opposition reflex to increase drive. Having a helper hold your dog back just before you throw or play with a toy, will make them want that toy just that little bit more.

Chase Method

The Chase method is something that we've covered a fair bit as well, but to briefly recap this is simply tossing a toy in the air for your dog to reach for, and catch before landing. Once this skill is transferred to the pool, this will encourage them to reach for a toy. The further you throw the more your dog will reach for it, and the more distance they will get in their jump. Be sure to throw some motivational throws that they *do* catch, or they will quit trying.

© Mahalia Goodey, Prairie Echo Photography

Finding The Right Toy

Sometimes you really have to play around to find what the right toy for your dog is, and what motivates them. Tennis balls are common water toys for the lake, but often are not a great choice because as your dog tries to bite them (especially the rubber ones) they slip away.

Using my previous example of Tess, she seemed to like tennis balls best but our normal Chuckit! Ultra Ball was too slippery for her to grab onto, so I thought I'd try the Chuckit! Hyrdo Squeeze Ball. It has a slippery surface but it has gaps with an absorbent material inside to help it float. She loves it, and it is easier for her to grab. I've started to introduce the Chuckit! Hydro Squeeze Bumper and that's gone well so far. Eventually we'll work to the Nerf Competition Stick and some other bumper style toys. For now though, this is great in between step to build her drive.

© Mahalia Goodey, Prairie Echo Photography

That being said my other dog Riggs can't play with those toys, he'd destroy them. So, you really need to know your dog - and don't be afraid to experiment a little bit. I know it sounds rich coming from somebody who has a pet store that sells toys, but whether you buy from me or not, that's the simple truth. I can't tell you how many toys I've gone through only to have my dogs turn up their nose at them

Tess also really loves her Kong Aqua, again it's a little more slippery, so we could try the Kong Wubba. The Wubba is a great ball like alternative that has a bit more of a grip, so your dog can quickly pick it up and be successful.

If you are competing in North America Diving Dogs, your dog is required to compete using a Nerf Competition Stick for the Air Retrieve and Hydro Dash. The earlier you can introduce your dog to the Nerf Competition Stick the better.

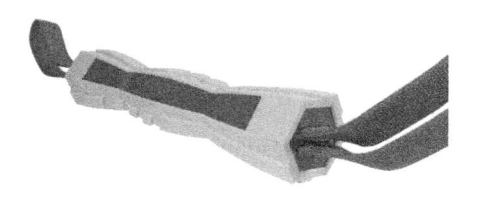

© Megan Ritchie

It's not a toy that most dogs intuitively love since it's on the harder side. If your dog is already interested in playing with bumpers it probably isn't going to be much of an issue. However, for more selective dogs it might take some training to get them playing with this required toy.

Now what?

Thanks for sticking with me through all the nitty gritty training details; I really hope this book is helpful to you when starting your dog. Nothing makes me happier than seeing you try this sport with new found confidence and showing off your hard work and success. Dock diving is an amazingly fun sport, and I hope this book helps make it a positive experience for you and your dog. Not to mention, saving you from the pitfalls and stumbles I've made.

If you found that helpful, you're going to want to get started training right away.

You've requested this book. You're still reading it. You've listened to everything I've said, and you know that if you start to use these training tips, you're going to have huge success in dock diving; and that's why you're going to want to check out our new Jumpstart Package.

If you want to know:

- What toys you need to have to get started
- When it's ok to force your dog into the pool
- What to do if your dog doesn't jump from the dock
- How to fit a life jacket and why you should use one with your dog
- Why all dogs can benefit from using a life jacket, even if they already know how to swim
- How to start dock diving, even if you don't have access to a pool
- You need to have a retriever, right? Wrong!
- Know the three things to look for in the best natural place to train
- How to eliminate hesitation
- You need to have a dog that loves toys, right? Wrong!
- The #1 thing you should never do when introducing the dock to your dog
- When it's ok for your dog to bite
- How to dock dive, even if you haven't done any dog training before
- Why retrievers might not be the best dog for dock diving
- How to say goodbye to a dog that doesn't swim

We've covered a little bit of this here already, but we're going to be able to cover it in a lot more detail in our Jumpstart Package with more video and photo resources, and a whole lot more information that didn't make the book. So, if you're interested in learning even more about dock diving and how to get started and compete, we've created this Jumpstart Package just for you.

What's included?

Well, it's pretty hard to play without some great floating toys, so we wanted to give you the three best toys for introducing your dog to dock diving:

- Kong Wubba ($24 Value)
- ChuckIt! Amphibious Bumper ($21 Value)
- ChuckIt! Zipflight ($22 Value)
- **Total $67 Value**

Kong Wubba

The Wubba has a neoprene exterior, which helps the toy float higher in the water. It also allows your dog to get a better grip than a standard tennis ball. Which means your tennis ball loving dog is going to have a lot of success right away in the pool, and will quickly learn to love this game.

ChuckIt! Amphibious Bumper

This is a really great bumper to introduce dock diving with. It's made of a nylon style material, with a soft foam core. A lot of dogs struggle starting with really hard hunting style bumpers. So, this softer material is a lot more appealing for them to learn with. However, it's still a very balanced toy, which means it's easy for you to throw and place exactly where you need to encourage your dog.

It floats high in the water; the orange version is very easy for your dog to see. It's also a little narrower than most hunting bumpers, so your dog isn't going to end up taking on as much water, which means a reduced risk of water poisoning, sputtering, and burping up water – which means more playing time.

ChuckIt! Zipflight

The third toy we've included is the ChuckIt! Zipflight. This is a great option to work towards Air Retrieve, especially for dogs that already play disc. We've tested a few discs and fell in love with the Zipflight. It's heavier than most floating discs, making it easier for you to throw over the relatively shorter pool distances without it being blown off course due to the wind.

Those are our top three recommended toys to introduce dock diving to your dog. We recommend all three if you're just starting because sometimes it does take a little trial and error to find the right toy for your dog; and sometimes your dog will show a different preference depending on the training drill you're working on.

This package gives you that flexibility, without making you spend a lot of money on toys that don't work (like I had to!).

Of course, the toys alone are only half the story! We couldn't let you walk away without some training and competition resources that would really help you to succeed.

So, as an added bonus, you'll also get access to:

The Quick Start Dock Diving System

Over five hours of training videos and resources so you'll know how to:

- Find the right toy for your dog (and you!)
- Know how to fit a life jacket for your dog, and how to use it
- What to expect the first time you go to a pool
- How to solve common training mistakes
- Association Resources
- Games Guide
- How to register with NADD and enter your first trial
- Where to go when you get there
- What to bring with you to your first trial
- Mindset tips for competing
- And lots more…

Total Value $197

To summarize, the Jumpstart Package includes:

Three awesome dock diving toys ($67 Value)

Bonus: The Quick Start Dock Diving System ($197 Value)

Total Value: $264

But of course, we're not going to ask you to pay that.

We're going to give you all of that for *just $67*.

And in case you're still thinking this might not be the real deal. If for any reason you don't like it, and don't think you got your money's worth, we're going to give you a 30-day money back guarantee. No questions asked, just send us an email within the first 30 days and let us know.

You don't even have to send the toys back.

Since we are really dedicated to having you succeed, we've also decided to include one more bonus! So, with this Jumpstart Package you're also going to receive our seven step Dock Diving Blueprint. The Blueprint will simplify everything in this book, and give you a step-by-step training plan so you'll know exactly what to work on and when.

How's that for over delivering?

So just to recap, you're going to receive:

Jumpstart Package

(Kong Wubba, Chuckit! Bumper, Chuckit! Zipflight) $67 Value

Bonus #1: The Quick Start Dock Diving System

(Over five hours of training videos & resources) $197 Value

Bonus #2: Dock Diving Blueprint

(Seven Step Training Blueprint) $37 Value

~~Total Value: $301~~

But you are receiving all of this for $67.

Of course, we can't make this offer forever, it does end. In order to focus on getting you up and running with our Jumpstart Package, we only offer it once a month at most, and typically only over the summer months. So, if you miss it now, you're going to miss a good chunk of the summer to get started.

Act now while you can, and take advantage of this ridiculous offer. Get started and play this wickedly fun game with your dog. We really want to make sure we help you out, so we keep this offer open for a very limited time. That way we can focus on you in our private Facebook group answering any questions you might have, and of course rush all this material to you as quickly as possible.

So, if you're really committed to training and having fun dock diving with your dog this summer, order your Jumpstart Package now and get started.

Resources:

Find All Links at:

www.myhighdrivedog.com/tactics

Association Links:

- North America Diving Dogs
- Dock Dogs
- Ultimate Air Dogs
- Splash Dogs

AKC Videos

1. Dock Diving
2. Ramp Work
3. Jumping Off The Dock
4. Prevent Hesitation
5. Chase Method
6. Throwing A Toy
7. Keep Practicing

Made in the USA
Monee, IL
17 December 2023